Seasoning Secrets

Flavor Booster Marinades, Rubs, Glazes & Sauces for Meat and Fish

By Jason Ortega

Your Free Gift

I wanted to show my appreciation that you support my work so I've put together a free gift for you.

[LIFESTYLE HACKS](http://gobigamz.com/instant-gifts-2/)

Just visit the link above to download it now.

I know you will love this gift.

Thanks!

Jason Ortega

Text Copyright © **Jason Ortega**

All rights reserved. No part of this guide may be reproduced in any form without permission in writing from the publisher except in the case of brief quotations embodied in critical articles or reviews.

Legal & Disclaimer

The information contained in this book and its contents is not designed to replace or take the place of any form of medical or professional advice; and is not meant to replace the need for independent medical, financial, legal or other professional advice or services, as may be required. The content and information in this book has been provided for educational and entertainment purposes only.

The content and information contained in this book has been compiled from sources deemed reliable, and it is accurate to the best of the Author's knowledge, information and belief. However, the Author cannot guarantee its accuracy and validity and cannot be held liable for any errors and/or omissions. Further, changes are periodically made to this book as and when needed. Where appropriate and/or necessary, you must consult a professional (including but not limited to your doctor, attorney, financial advisor or such other professional advisor) before using any of the suggested remedies, techniques, or information in this book.

Upon using the contents and information contained in this book, you agree to hold harmless the Author from and against any damages, costs, and expenses, including any legal fees potentially resulting from the application of any of the information provided by this book. This disclaimer applies to any loss, damages or injury caused by the use and application, whether directly or indirectly, of any advice or information presented, whether for breach of contract, tort, negligence, personal injury, criminal intent, or under any other cause of action.

You agree to accept all risks of using the information presented inside this book.

You agree that by continuing to read this book, where appropriate and/or necessary, you shall consult a professional (including but not limited to your doctor, attorney, or financial advisor or such other advisor as needed) before using any of the suggested remedies, techniques, or information in this book.

Table of Contents

INTRODUCTION
- MESMERIZING MARINADES
- THE SPICED WORLD OF RUBS
- GLAMOROUS GLAZES
- SCRUMPTIOUS SAUCES

CHAPTER ONE

MOUTH MUMBLING MEAT & FISH MARINADES

AMAZING ALL-SEASON MEAT MARINADES
- TANGY MOJITO MARINADE
- BEST EVER HONEY KABOB MARINADE
- THAI STYLE COCONUT SOY MARINADE
- ITALIAN STYLE PARSLEY & BASIL MARINADE
- SAVORY PEANUT BUTTER MARINADE
- SOY HONEY BALSAMIC MARINADE
- ROSEMARY OLIVE STEAK MARINADE
- PINEAPPLE MARINADE TWIST

AMAZING ALL-SEASON FISH MARINADES
- TANGY MEDITERRANEAN MARINADE
- SUPER SESAME SALMON MARINADE
- WHITE WINE MUSTARD MARINADE
- JALAPEÑO OREGANO MARINADE
- GORGEOUS GREEN HERB MARINADE

CHAPTER TWO

MESMERIZING MEAT AND FISH GLAZES

AMAZING ALL-SEASON MEAT GLAZES
- CHIPOTLE BLUEBERRY GLAZE
- AWESOME APRICOT CORNSTARCH GLAZE
- SPECIAL WHISKY MEAT GLAZE
- SCRUMPTIOUS CRANBERRY GLAZE
- ASIAN STYLE SESAME SEED MEAT GLAZE
- FRUITY MUSTARD HAM GLAZE
- SMOOTH SOY HONEY GLAZE
- APPLE SPICED MEAT GLAZE
- JALAPEÑO COKE GLAZE
- CORN CRANBERRY GLAZE

AMAZING ALL-SEASON FISH GLAZES
- CLASSIC HONEY MUSTARD FISH GLAZE
- MAPLE SYRUP SPICED FISH GLAZE

Teriyaki Tangy Fish Glaze

CHAPTER THREE

EXTRA SCRUMPTIOUS SUPER MEAT & FISH RUBS

AMAZING ALL-SEASON MEAT RUBS

- Tunisian Mixed Spiced Rub
- All Purpose Dill Seed Rub
- Rosemary Thyme Rub
- Super Spiced Curry Rub
- Mexican Cocoa Rub
- Juniper Sage Meat Rub
- Southwestern Oregano Thyme Rub
- Tangy Pepper & Thyme Rub

AMAZING ALL-SEASON FISH RUBS

- Oregano Cumin Tilapia Rub
- Spicy Sumac Rub
- Lemon Pepper Coriander Rub
- Long Island Spiced Rub

CHAPTER FOUR

THE AMAZING WORLD OF MEAT & FISH SUPER SAUCES

AMAZING ALL-SEASON MEAT SAUCES

- Super Salsa Sauce with Mint and Anchovies
- Mustard Mushroom Beef Sauce
- Creamy Horseradish Chicken Sauce
- Creamy Peppercorn Steak Sauce
- Tangy Beef Oregano Sauce
- Spiced Black Bean Sauce
- Cheesy Nutty Chicken Sauce
- Peanut Coconut Cream Sauce

AMAZING ALL-SEASON FISH SAUCES

- Ginger Tomatino Saucy Feast
- Bercy White Wine Sauce
- Fresh Tarragon Parsley Sauce
- Normandy Nostalgia Sauce

CONCLUSION

Introduction

Seasoning - Some call it an art, some call it an essential kitchen skill; there are many names, but the end purpose remains the same: producing a perfectly moist and flavor blended meat and fish to make outrageously delicious cuisines at home. It's all about enhancing the flavors to delight your taste buds.

The world of seasoning is quite broad and involves so many unique methods; in this "Seasoning Secrets" book, I will be focusing on some of the most popular seasoning styles to flavor up your meats as well as fish cuisines.

Mesmerizing Marinades

In most cultures, marinades are popularly referred as a surface treatment. It is all about penetrating a delicious combination of flavorful ingredients into your meat cuts and varieties of fish.

This amazing technique beautifully tenderizes them and makes them heavenly scrumptious. Variety of acids, oils along with seasoning ingredients, is essential components for most marinades.

Marinating Tips:

- Your meat cuts or fish need to be soaked in the prepared marinade; you can either marinate at room temperature or they can be placed in the refrigerator for minimum 30 minutes. Maximum time to marinate can be 8 hours, 12 hours and even more depending on the ingredients used, and type of meat or fish used.

- After the soaking time is over, do not throw away the mixture as you can brush it over entrees for additional flavoring.

- Marinade recipes are also great to flavor up your burgers. So, apart from using it to marinate meats and fish, also experiment by adding in your burgers.

The Spiced World of Rubs

The world of rubs is filled with variety of spices, herbs, and other healthy ingredients. Be it a professional cook or a beginner, savory rubs are there to make your meal extra spicy and flavorful. They are popular to prepare weekend meals as well as summer barbeques. To be honest, they are great to prepare delicious meals for any given day.

Application Tips:

- Your meat cuts or fish need to be lightly coated with olive oil before you start applying the prepared rub mixture, as it makes the rub application process seamless. Also, it helps in creating a moisture lock, as well as helps the ingredients to firmly stick with meat/fish surface.

- Many rub recipes consist of dry ingredients. Now, if you prefer to make it a little moist and wish to give it a paste-like texture, you can add a few drops of olive oil. In case of preparing fish, it will prevent fish from sticking to grill grates.

- When applying a rub to prepare grilled meats or fish, apply it at least 30-40 minutes prior to grilling time for optimum flavor absorption.

Glamorous Glazes

Glazes add glamour to your food along with world of flavors; they craft your cuisines with attractive finishing and give them a perfect glossy touch. In many ways, glazes and meat cuts/fish complement each other wonderfully.

Useful Tips:

- In most cases, glazes are applied during the terminal phase of a specified cooking time. However, it is not a ground rule, as many recipes need glaze application at the start of a recipe making.

- The reason for glazing your foods during the terminal phase is in its sugar content. The sugar may burn completely and can affect the taste of your favorite meals.

- Glazes are also great to be served as dipping sauces. Make a practice of preparing a large quantity to glaze your desired meat or fish and then reserve some quantity to enjoy as a dipping sauce.

Scrumptious Sauces

Sauces are there to add perfection to your juicy, flavorful meats and fish. Homemade sauces let you explore your creativity and create your own collection of customized sauces with your unique set of ingredients.

Sauces make perfect companion to enjoy grilled meats and fish, roasts, and chops. Try out different sets of combos and flavors to complement your meats and fish. They form essential part to enjoy recipes with mild flavors to balance out the overall taste and flavors.

Chapter ONE
Mouth Mumbling Meat & Fish Marinades

It's time to master the art of making scrumptious meat marinades! Time is the essence, when it comes to preparing perfectly moist marinades. Make sure to follow the timelines when prepping your choice of marinades:

Chicken and pork varieties

- Recommended time: 30 minutes to 12 hours

- If time permits, marinate for more hours or overnight, as it will make your pork and chicken tender.

Beef and lamb varieties

- Recommended time: 30 minutes to 24 hours

Fish varieties

- Recommended time: 30-60 minutes

- Do not marinate for more than an hour, as it will make the fish mushy.

Amazing All-Season Meat Marinades

Tangy Mojito Marinade

This unique tangy marinade is made from a refreshing combination of muddled sugar, fresh mint, rum, and lime juice (the most popular term for this combination is "mojito"). It's a uniquely delicious choice of marinade to prepare shrimp, chicken, mahi-mahi, pork, as well as tofu at home.

Prep. Time: 8-10 min.

Total Time: 10 min.

Yield: 2-cups/16 oz.

Ingredients:

- Fresh mint, chopped - 1/4 cup
- Shallots, peel and trim thoroughly - 2

- Rum - 1/4 cup
- Honey - 3 tbs.
- Lime juice - 1/2 cup
- Canola oil - 2 tbs.
- Kosher salt - 1 tbs.

Directions:

You need a food processor or blender to make this minty marinade; one by one, add oil, lime zest, honey, lime juice, rum, mint, shallots, and salt.

First, blend or process using "pulse" mode for a few minutes to finely chop the shallots. Then, take your baking dish; add the mixture into it. You can also use sealable plastic bag with 1-gallon capacity instead of baking dish.

Put your chosen meat in the bag or baking dish; mix it to coat evenly.

Place the marinade meat mixture to refrigerate; give the meat marinade mixture adequate time to soak flavors.

Best Ever Honey Kabob Marinade

Transform your Kabob fantasy into a memorable dining experience; it is a perfectly sweet & healthy marinade to prepare pork and chicken.

You can experiment on your own by adding your choice of ingredients like portabella mushrooms, onions or zucchini while preparing the meals with this honey-marinated meat.

Prep. Time: 5 min.

Total Time: 10 min.

Yield: 1 1/2-Cup/12 oz.

Ingredients:

- Soy sauce - 1/2 cup
- Honey - 1/2 cup
- Chili tomato sauce - 1/4 cup
- Vegetable oil - 2 tbs.
- Ground cumin as required

Directions:

To prepare the kabob marinade, first take your bowl of medium to large size; one by one, add in the soy sauce, honey, tomato sauce, oil, and cumin. Mix them all well.

Add your chosen meat in the marinade mixture; mix it to coat evenly.

Refrigerate the kabob marinade mixture for the required time to marinate nicely.

Thai Style Coconut Soy Marinade

Coconut milk infused marinades are a fantastic choice to make richly flavored tender chicken. This garlic and soy sauce infused marinade with give bright punch to your dinner meals. It also makes a suitable choice of meals for seasonal parties.

Prep. Time: 5 min.

Total Time: 8-10 min.

Yield: ½ cup/4 oz.

Ingredients:

- Brown sugar - 1 tbs.
- Soy sauce - 1/2 tsp.

- Light coconut milk - 1/4 cup + extra 2 tbs.
- Garlic clove, large size and roughly chopped – 1
- Chopped fresh ginger - 1 inch long piece
- Fresno or Thai chili pepper, slice it thinly - 1

Directions:

To prepare the Thai marinade, first take your bowl of medium to large size; one by one, add in all mentioned ingredients in it. Mix them all well.

Add your chosen meat in the marinade mixture; mix it to coat evenly.

Place the marinade meat mixture to refrigerate. Give the meat marinade mixture adequate time to soak flavors.

Italian Style Parsley & Basil Marinade

This Italian style marinade will transform your chicken sinfully delicious. Mixed with parsley, garlic and basil, it will be a unique addition to your collection of herb-based healthy marinades.

Prep. Time: 5 min.

Total Time: 7-8 min.

Yield: ¾ cup/6 oz.

Ingredients:

- Balsamic vinegar - 1/4 cup
- Olive oil - 1/4 cup
- Garlic clove, large size and roughly chopped – 1

- Minced fresh basil - 1 tbs.
- Minced fresh parsley - 1 tbs.
- Red chili flakes - 1/2 tsp.

Directions:

To prepare the marinade, take your bowl of medium to large size; one by one, add in the mentioned marinade ingredients. Mix them all well.

Add your chosen meat in the marinade mixture; mix it to coat evenly. Place it in the refrigerator.

Savory Peanut Butter Marinade

Hailed from classic Asian ingredients, this premium marinade also makes a yummy choice for sauce. Peanut butter marinades add a unique sweetness to beef of chicken meals. I made it last weekend for the whole family and it's simply sensational!

Prep. Time: 5 min.

Total Time: 8-10 min.

Yield: 1 ¾ cup/14 oz.

Ingredients:

- Soy sauce - 1/4 cup
- Creamy peanut butter - 1/2 cup

- Hot water - 1/2 cup
- Chile paste - 1/4 cup
- White vinegar - 2 tbs.
- Vegetable oil - 2 tbs.
- Garlic, minced - 4 cloves
- Ground red pepper - 1/4 tsp.
- Grated fresh ginger root - 2 tsp.

Directions:

To prepare peanut butter marinade, take your bowl of medium to large size; then, add hot water and peanut butter. Mix it well in the water.

One by one, add in the remaining ingredients. Mix them all well.

Add the beef or chicken in the marinade mixture; mix it to coat evenly. Refrigerate the meat marinade mixture for about 12-14 hours to marinate nicely.

Soy Honey Balsamic Marinade

This tangy, dark marinade can be used to infuse lovely flavors to different varieties of beef. It's a little salty and filled with rich flavor.

As this is a multipurpose marinade, you can also drizzle it over your favorite choice of salads.

Prep. Time: 5 min.

Total Time: 5 min.

Yield: 1 cup/8 oz.

Ingredients:

- Soy sauce - ¼ cup
- Balsamic vinegar - 1/2cup

- Honey - 2 tbs.
- Crushed red pepper - ½ tsp.
- Scallions, chopped – 4 pieces

Directions:

To prepare the soy marinade, take your bowl of medium to large size; one by one, add in all mentioned marinade ingredients. Mix them all well.

Add your chosen variety of beef in the marinade mixture; mix it to coat evenly.

Place the marinade beef mixture to refrigerate. Give the mixture adequate time (minimum 30 minutes or overnight) to soak flavors.

Rosemary Olive Steak Marinade

Zesty concoctions of this unique olive marinade will perfectly tenderize your favorite steak. Let the ingredients perfectly infuse the steak to spread more smiles and experience the real joy of healthy marinated foods.

Prep. Time: 5 min.

Total Time: 8-10 min.

Yield: Perfect quantity to prepare 32 oz. steak

Ingredients:

- Olive oil – 2 tbs.
- Red wine vinegar - ½ cup
- Bay leaf - 1
- Chopped fresh rosemary – 2 tbs.
- Garlic cloves, chopped - 4

- Chopped fresh oregano – 2 tbs.
- Black pepper and salt as required

Directions:

To prepare the rosemary marinade, take your bowl of medium to large size; one by one, add in all mentioned marinade ingredients. Mix them all well.

Add the steak in the marinade mixture; mix it to coat evenly.

Place the steak mixture to refrigerate. Give the mixture adequate time (minimum 30 minutes or overnight) to soak flavors.

Pineapple Marinade Twist

No matter how hard I try, I couldn't stop myself from pining over some juicy and fruity pork dishes. One fine afternoon, I decided to bring home some pineapples from the nearby fruit market and try them out in this soy sauce-based marinade.

The fruity taste of pineapple creates magic in this special pork marinade. Try it yourself at home as soon as you can.

Prep. Time: 10 min.

Total Time: 10 min.

Yield: 1 cup/8 oz.

Ingredients:

- Soy sauce - ⅓ cup
- Crushed pineapple - 1 cup
- Powdered cloves - ½ tsp.
- Honey - ⅓ cup

- Cloves garlic, minced - 2
- Cider vinegar - ¼ cup
- Ginger powder - 1 tsp.

Directions:

To prepare the pineapple marinade, take your bowl of medium to large size; one by one, add in all mentioned marinade ingredients. Mix them all well.

Put the pork in the marinade mixture; mix it to coat evenly.

Refrigerate the pork marinade mixture for the required time to marinate nicely.

Amazing All-Season Fish Marinades

Tangy Mediterranean Marinade

Tangy Mediterranean marinade deliciously infuses all kinds of fish varieties including swordfish and salmon. This classic Mediterranean recipe is full of citrus flavors and fresh herbs including parsley, cumin, coriander, and garlic. An ideal choice of marinade to make a hot, savory BBQ fish meal!

Prep. Time: 5 min.

Total Time: 30-45 min.

Yield: 1 ¼ cup/11 oz.

Ingredients:

- Fresh coriander, finely chopped - 4 tbs.
- Fresh parsley, finely chopped - 4 tbs.

- Juice of 1 lime
- Fresh lemon juice - 6 tbs.
- Garlic, crushed – 3 cloves
- Cumin - 2 tsp.
- Paprika - 4 tsp.
- Black pepper - 1 tsp.

Directions:

To prepare the fish marinade, first take your bowl or baking dish of medium to large size; one by one, add in the mentioned marinade ingredients. Whisk them all well.

You can also use sealable plastic bag with 1-gallon capacity instead of baking dish.

Now, add the fish in the marinade mixture; mix it to coat evenly. Give the mixture around 30 minutes to soak flavors.

Super Sesame Salmon Marinade

Reserve your weekend meal schedule in advance to cook salmon infused with this super sesame marinade at home. You will find hundreds of ideas for salmon marinades, but this healthy and yummy marinade will outrank every one of them. Try it out and it will be your every weekend affair!

Prep. Time: 5 min.

Total Time: 8-10 min.

Yield: 1 cup/8 oz.

Ingredients:

- Soy sauce - 2 tbs.

- Olive oil - ¼ cup
- Rice vinegar - 2 tbs.
- Brown sugar - 2 tbs.
- Sesame oil - 2 tbs.
- Garlic, pressed – 2 cloves
- Sesame seeds - 1 tbs.
- Grated fresh ginger - 1 tbs.
- Green onions, thinly sliced - 4

Directions:

To prepare the sesame marinade, first take your bowl of medium to large size; one by one add in the mentioned marinade ingredients. Mix them all well.

You can also use sealable plastic bag with 1-gallon capacity instead of baking dish.

Add your fish/salmon in the marinade mixture; mix it to coat evenly. Give the mixture around 30 minutes to soak flavors.

White Wine Mustard Marinade

A true fish and wine lover cannot say "no" to this perfectly formed marinade with variety of flavors; addition of mustard power and red onion greatly deepens its flavor profile. The time is perfect to jazz up your evenings with this classy mustard-based fish marinade.

Prep. Time: 15 min.

Total Time: 20 min.

Yield: 2 ¾ cup/23 oz.

Ingredients:

- Lime Juice - 1/2 cup

- White Wine - 1 3/4 cups
- Mustard Powder - 1 1/2 tsp.
- Olive Oil - 1/2 cup
- Red Onion, sliced – 1 medium size piece
- Pepper and salt as required

Directions:

To prepare the white wine marinade, take your bowl of medium to large size; one by one, add in all mentioned marinade ingredients. Mix them all well.

Refrigerate the marinade mixture overnight to set completely.

Take the bowl out; then, add the fish into the marinade mixture; mix it to coat evenly. Refrigerate for about 30 minutes to marinate nicely.

Jalapeño Oregano Marinade

Be it hectic weekdays or soothing weekend nights, white wine-marinated fish makes a divine meal to have on any day.

Fresh Jalapeño mixed with oregano leaves provides a spiced kick to this special fish marinade recipe. Excellent choice to marinate your favorite salmon, swordfish as well as mahi-mahi!

Prep. Time: 10 min.

Total Time: 15 min.

Yield: 2-¼-cup/18 oz.

Ingredients:

- Jalapeño Chilies, diced - 8 oz.
- Oregano Leaves - 3 tbsp.
- White Wine - 1 1/2 cups
- Olive Oil - 1/3 cup

Directions:

You need a food processor or blender to make this jalapeño marinade; one by one, add in the oil (2 tbs.), chilies, wine (12 cup), and oregano. Blend or process it using "pulse" mode for few minutes.

Then, take your baking dish and add the mixture in it. You can also use sealable plastic bag with 1-gallon capacity instead of baking dish.

Mix in remaining wine and oil. Mix again.

Now add the fish in the marinade mixture; mix it to coat evenly. Refrigerate for about 30 minutes to marinate nicely.

Gorgeous Green Herb Marinade

Get ready to experience some Italian flavors in your fish-based meals with this green herb marinade; rosemary and yellow onion provide a classic touch to it. Make it at home and discover a zesty and vibrant combination of flavors!

Prep. Time: 5 min.

Total Time: 8-10 min.

Yield: 3-½-cups/22 oz.

Ingredients:

- Fresh basil leaves - 1 cup
- Yellow onion, coarsely chopped -1 medium size
- Italian parsley - 1/2 cup

- Fresh sage leaves - 1 tbsp.
- Rosemary leaves - 2 tbsp.
- Lemon juice - 1 tbsp.
- Lemon zest - 1 tbsp.
- Capers, medium to large size - 2 tbsp.
- Olive oil - 1 cup
- Garlic cloves, peeled - 4
- Fresh mint - 1/2 tsp.
- Pepper and salt as required

Directions:

You need a food processor or blender to make this green herb marinade; one by one, add in the herbs, onion, lemon zest, garlic, lemon juice, and capers. Blend or process all using "pulse" mode for a few minutes.

Then mix in the pepper, salt, and oil. Blend again to make the puree.

Then, take your baking dish; add the mixture in it. You can also use sealable plastic bag with 1-gallon capacity instead of baking dish.

Now, add the fish in the marinade mixture; mix it to coat evenly. Refrigerate for about 30 minutes to marinate nicely.

Chapter TWO
Mesmerizing Meat and Fish Glazes

Perk up your meat fantasies with the best glazes you can ever find. They are amazing flavor enhancers, be it pork chops, ham, chicken, beef, salmon, or your favorite variety of fish.

Amazing All-Season Meat Glazes

Chipotle Blueberry Glaze

This incredible fruity glaze beautifully combines the spiciness of chipotle with the sweet and tangy taste of blueberries. Blueberries infuse the recipe with digestion-aiding properties; moreover, they are also loaded with cholesterol-controlling manganese and health boosting vitamin C.

I have used blueberries in making varieties of pies, cakes, ice creams, and fruit pizzas; now it's time to make a unique glaze from them.

Prep. Time: 30-35 min.

Total Time: 40 min.

Yield: 5-6 cups

Ingredients:

- Brown sugar - 1/2 cup
- Water - 1 3/4 cup
- Frozen blueberries - 4 cups
- Thyme - 4 sprigs
- Rosemary - 1 sprig
- Honey - 1 to 2 tbs.
- Black pepper and salt as required

Directions:

To make the meat glaze, combine sugar and water in your medium-sized saucepan. Let the mixture boil gradually.

Then, mix honey, pepper, salt, herbs, and berries in the hot pan mixture; gently stir it. Allow 25-30 minutes to simmer the mixture.

Cook your favorite meat cuts in the same saucepan. Gently spread or pour the prepared glaze over the cuts during the last few minutes of your cooking time.

Flip halfway through; let the cuts get completely glazed from both the sides and absorb its moist flavors. Enjoy the blueberry-glazed meal!

Awesome Apricot Cornstarch Glaze

For the past few weeks, I have been thinking to be creative and came up with my own version of ham glaze; so, I decided to experiment with cornstarch and apricot nectar. The result was unexpectedly fulfilling along with a huge proud smile on my face.

This special apricot glaze was created exclusively to glaze ham cuts, but it also beautifully glazes beef and pork cuts filling them with vibrant flavors.

Prep. Time: 5 min.

Total Time: 8-10 min.

Yield: 1 ½ cup/12 oz.

Ingredients:

- Cornstarch - 1 tbs.
- Brown sugar, packed - 1 tbs.

- Ginger - 1/2 tsp.
- Apricot nectar - 1 can of 12 oz.
- Salt - 1/4 tsp.
- Lemon juice - 1 tbs.

Directions:

To make this apricot glaze, combine ginger, cornstarch, salt, and sugar in your medium-sized saucepan. Gently stir them all.

Then, mix in the lemon juice and nectar. Mix again and let the mixture boil gradually. Allow 2-3 minutes to simmer the mixture, to make it thick.

Now, take your favorite cooked/grilled/baked meat cuts. Gently spread or pour the prepared glaze over the cuts. Allow few minutes for the glaze to set in.

The savory apricot glazed meat is ready to serve. Enjoy warm!

Special Whisky Meat Glaze

If you are a steak freak like me, craving for juicy steak on TGI Fridays, then you can't afford to miss out on this one. It is, indeed, the perfect choice to glaze chicken, fish, and pork varieties.

Make it for your whole family and it will leave everyone fulfilled and jittery! No one can resist the magic of its lip-smacking whisky-infused flavors.

Prep. Time: 35 min.

Total Time: 40 min.

Yield: 1 ½ cup/12 oz.

Ingredients:

- Pineapple, finely minced - 3 to 4 Chunks
- White onion, minced – ½ piece

- Garlic, minced – 3 cloves
- Whiskey of your choice – 1.5 oz./50 ml
- Lemon Juice - 2 tsp.
- Light Soya Sauce - 1 tsp.
- Brown Sugar - 4 tbsp.
- Water – 5 oz.
- Cayenne Pepper - 1/4 tsp.
- Pineapple Juice – 7 oz.
- Teriyaki Sauce – 1.5 oz./50 ml
- Olive Oil – 1 tsp.

Directions:

To make this whiskey meat glaze, combine the garlic, onion, and oil in your medium-sized saucepan. Cook them for 3-4 minutes.

Now, mix in the sugar, juice, and water. Let the mixture boil gradually.

Then, mix in the sauces, pineapple chunks, pepper, whiskey, and lemon juice. Allow 25-30 minutes to simmer the mixture.

The savory whiskey glaze is ready to serve over your favorite meat cuts. Enjoy warm!

Scrumptious Cranberry Glaze

To be honest, I was little hesitant to make this cranberry glaze, as I was always afraid to sail new seas. But after realizing how scrumptious this glaze can make varieties of meat cuts, I am ready to venture into unique experiments. Mint and orange juice add a nice tang to your glazed meat meals.

Prep. Time: 25 min.

Total Time: 30 min.

Yield: 1 ½ cup/12 oz.

Ingredients:

- Fresh mint sprigs, crushed - 1/4 oz.
- Honey - 1/2 cup
- Orange juice - 1 cup
- Dried cranberries - 1/3 cup

Directions:

To make the cranberry meat glaze, combine berries and orange juice in your medium-sized saucepot. Let the mixture boil gradually.

Allow 15-20 minutes to simmer the mixture. Now, mix in the honey and sprigs. Continue to simmer for about 8-10 minutes. Discard the sprigs.

Now, take your favorite cooked/grilled/baked meat cuts. Gently spread or pour the prepared glaze over the cuts. Allow a few minutes for the glaze to set in. Enjoy the cranberry-glazed meal!

Asian Style Sesame Seed Meat Glaze

Wondering what special recipe to make on upcoming holiday season? Be it a New Year's Eve, Thanksgiving or Christmas, add this one for sure to your holiday meat recipe list.

Sesame seeds along with ginger and garlic nicely improve the texture and the look of the meat cuts. Reserve it for special occasions and parties; it's a sure shot party hit recipe to entice your guests!

Prep. Time: 10 min.

Total Time: 15 min.

Yield: 2-½-cup/16 oz.

Ingredients:

- Soy sauce - 1 cup

- Roasted sesame seeds - 4 tbs.
- Brown sugar - 1 cup
- Salt - ¼ tsp.
- Garlic, minced - 3 cloves
- Fresh ginger, minced - 2 tsp.
- Sesame oil - 4 tbsp.
- Green onions, chopped – for garnishing

Directions:

To make the sesame meat glaze, combine the oil, ginger, soy sauce, garlic, salt, and sugar into your medium-sized saucepan. Let the mixture boil gradually for about 10 minutes. Now, mix in the seeds in the pan.

Then, take your favorite cooked/grilled/baked meat cuts. Gently spread or pour the prepared glaze over the cuts. Allow a few minutes for the glaze to set in. Garnish with green onions on top. Enjoy the sesame seed glazed meal!

Fruity Mustard Ham Glaze

This super easy mustard ham glaze requires only four ingredients to brush magic on your favorite ham or pork chops. Pineapple juice provides sweet and tangy touch along with the unique taste of mustard; addition of honey brings an undated twist to your glazed pork of ham meal.

Prep. Time: 5 min.

Total Time: 8-10 min.

Yield: ¾ cup/6 oz.

Ingredients:

- Pineapple juice - 1 tbs.
- Honey - 3 tbs.
- Brown sugar, packed - ½ cup
- Dijon mustard - 1 tbs.

Directions:

To make this meat glaze, combine all mentioned glaze ingredients in your medium-sized bowl. Gently blend the ingredients.

Cook your favorite meat cuts in a skillet of medium to large size. Gently spread or pour the prepared glaze over the cuts during the last few minutes of your cooking time.

If you are baking the meat cuts, then glaze them by using a brush, then place them back to bake for about 40-45 minutes.

Smooth Soy Honey Glaze

Both soy sauce and honey are known for their nourishing properties; the nutritious combo is a valuable healthy addition to pork chops or steak, chicken, and baby back ribs.

You can garnish them with your choice of ingredients including sesame seeds, coriander, etc. for a complete makeover.

Prep. Time: 5 min.

Total Time: 8-10 min.

Yield: 6 oz.

Ingredients:

- Low-sodium soy sauce - 2 tbs.
- Honey - ¼ cup

Directions:

To make this soy honey glaze, combine the mentioned glaze ingredients in your medium-sized bowl. Gently blend the ingredients.

Grill the meat cuts in a skillet of medium to large size, then glaze them by using a brush; place them back to grill for about 8-10 minutes.

Flip halfway through; let the cuts get completely glazed from both the sides and absorb its moist flavors. Enjoy the soy honey glazed meal!

Apple Spiced Meat Glaze

This apple-spiced glaze is the one that made me drooled over and over again just by thinking of making it.

Cinnamon adds a touch of sweetness and deep character to any grilled or cooked meat. This savory spiced glaze is a perfect companion for your weekend dinner meals!

Prep. Time: 30 min.

Total Time: 35-40 min.

Yield: 1 ½ cup/12 oz.

Ingredients:

- Apple juice or cider - 1/4 cup
- Brown sugar, packed - 1 1/4 cups
- Flour - 2 tbs.
- Dry mustard - 1/2 tsp.

- Cinnamon - 1/2 tsp.
- Allspice mixture - 1/4 tsp.

Directions:

To make the apple-spiced glaze, combine all mentioned glaze ingredients in your medium-sized bowl. Gently blend the ingredients.

Cook your favorite meat cuts in a skillet of medium to large size. Gently spread or pour the prepared glaze over the cuts during the last few minutes of your cooking time.

If you are baking the meat cuts, then glaze them by using a brush; then, place them back to bake for about 40-45 minutes. Enjoy the spiced glazed meal!

Jalapeño Coke Glaze

Here is an easy and savory cola glaze recipe for your whole family. The Jalapeño chili and coke flavored glaze works like magic on any given meat cut; additionally, it delivers exceptional flavor boost to your favorite ham cut.

Prep. Time: 10 min.

Total Time: 12-15 min.

Yield: 1 1/2-Cups/12 oz.

Ingredients:

- Jalapeño chilies, cut to make thick slices of ¼ inch – 2 medium size pieces
- Lime juice - 1/4 cup
- Coke, diet or classic - 1 cup
- Light brown sugar - 2 cups

Directions:

To make the Coke meat glaze, combine the Jalapeños, sugar, Coke, and lime juice in your medium-sized saucepan. Let the mixture boil gradually for about 6-8 minutes.

Now, take your favorite cooked/grilled/baked meat cuts. Gently spread or pour the prepared glaze over the cuts. Allow a few minutes for the glaze to set in. Enjoy the Coke glazed meal!

Corn Cranberry Glaze

This easy to make corn cranberry glaze recipe is ideal to make quick glazed meat meals on Saturday afternoon to give you more leisure time to spend with your family and loved ones. A must-try glaze for cranberry lovers!

Prep. Time: 5 min.

Total Time: 8-10 min.

Yield: 1 cup/8 oz.

Ingredients:

- Light corn syrup - 1/2 cup
- Cranberry jelly (jam)- 1 cup

Directions:

To make this corn jelly meat glaze, combine the corn syrup and cranberry jelly in your medium-sized bowl. Gently blend the ingredients.

Now, take your favorite cooked/grilled/baked meat cuts. Gently spread or pour the prepared glaze over the cuts. Allow few minutes for the glaze to set in. Enjoy the jelly-glazed meal!

Amazing All-Season Fish Glazes

Classic Honey Mustard Fish Glaze

Complement your choice of fish including salmon by infusing it with succulent flavors and a perfectly glazed look by this classic honey mustard glaze.

Honey and mustard are versatile and fun, as they let you experiment endlessly and discover something new every time.

Prep. Time: 5 min.

Total Time: 8-10 min.

Yield: 1/2 cup/4 oz.

Ingredients:

- Dijon mustard - 2 tsp.
- Soy sauce (low sodium) - 4 tbsp.

- Honey - 6 tbsp.
- Lime juice - 2 tsp.

Directions:

To make the honey mustard fish glaze, combine the mustard, soy sauce, lime juice, and honey in your medium-sized bowl. Gently blend the ingredients.

Then, add the mixture into your medium-sized saucepan. Let the mixture simmer gradually for about 2 minutes.

Now, take your favorite cooked/grilled/baked salmon or any other fish variety. Gently spread or pour the prepared glaze over the fish/salmon. Allow a few minutes for the glaze to set in. Enjoy the mustard glazed fish meal!

Maple Syrup Spiced Fish Glaze

Give your parties and occasions a rich and classic upgrade with this maple syrup glaze. Nutmeg, combined with sharp flavors of cinnamon, makes this yummy fish glaze perfect to prepare holiday or seasonal meals.

Prep. Time: 5 min.

Total Time: 8-10 min.

Yield: 1 cup/8 oz.

Ingredients:

- Apple cider vinegar - 1/2 cup
- Apple cider - 1/2 cup
- Olive oil - 1 tbs.
- Brown sugar - 2 tbs.
- Maple syrup - 1 tbs.
- Cinnamon - 2 tsp.
- Salt - 1 tsp.
- Nutmeg - 1 tsp.
- Onion powder - 1/2 tsp.

Directions:

To make the maple syrup glaze, combine all mentioned fish marinade ingredients in your food processor or blender. Gently blend the ingredients.

Now, take your favorite cooked/grilled/baked baked salmon or any other fish variety. Gently spread or pour the prepared glaze over the cuts. Allow a few minutes for the glaze to set in. Enjoy the maple syrup-glazed fish meal!

Teriyaki Tangy Fish Glaze

Rice wine paired with tangy orange juice make it a perfect fish meal to have on any given day. This saucy Teriyaki glaze brings out the juicy, mild flavors of fish. Try out this on weekend and impress yourself!

Prep. Time: 5 min.

Total Time: 8-10 min.

Yield: 1 ¼ cup/10 oz.

Ingredients:

- Rice wine - 1/4 cup
- Orange juice, with pulp - 3/4 cup
- Soy sauce - 3 tbs.
- Minced scallions - 1 tbs.
- Honey - 1 tbs.
- Orange slices – for garnishing
- Lemon juice - 1 tsp.

Directions:

To make the teriyaki glaze, combine the mentioned fish marinade ingredients in your food processor or blender. Gently blend the ingredients.

Now, take your favorite cooked/grilled/baked baked salmon or any other fish variety. Gently spread or pour the prepared glaze over the cuts. Allow a few minutes for the glaze to set in. Enjoy the teriyaki glazed fish meal!

Chapter THREE
Extra Scrumptious Super Meat & Fish Rubs

Spice up your dream meats and fish with some extra flavors of the following handpicked collection of meat as well as fish rubs to put an end to your spicy food cravings.

Rubs – How Much is Adequate for your Meat?

- For meat cuts including steak, chicken, and pork, using rub mixture of 1 tbs. (3 tsp.) per 16 oz. piece is suggested.

- For variety of fish, rub mixture of ½ tbs. (1 to 2 tsp.) to 1 tbs. (3 tsp.) per 16 oz. piece is adequate.

- To be safe, use less quantity for the first time to determine its spice strength. You will be able to adjust the quantity next time.

Amazing All-Season Meat Rubs

Tunisian Mixed Spiced Rub

This incredible rub recipe hailed from the Tunisian cooking secrets; the rub is the essential seasoning base for variety of Tunisian dishes.

This lovely spice blend created by caraway seeds, coriander, and hot pepper works like a charm on your favorite pork tenderloin, chicken as well as salmon.

Prep. Time: 5 min.

Total Time: 8-10 min.

Yield: 5-½ tsp.

Ingredients:

- Coriander seeds - 2 tsp.
- Caraway seeds - 2 tsp.
- Crushed red pepper - 3/4 tsp.

- Garlic powder - 3/4 tsp.
- Kosher salt - 1/2 tsp.

Directions:

Mix in the coriander seeds, red pepper and caraway seeds in your spice blender, grinder or processor to make this rub. Start processing or blending the mixed spices on "pulse" mode mixture to ground.

Put the mixed spice mixture into a bowl; mix in the salt and garlic powder. Mix again well.

Now, take your choice of meat cut and place it on a firm surface. Brush or rub the freshly made rub on it; pat gently for the rub to stick onto the surface. Turn the meat cut and repeat to spice up its other side. Repeat with other meat cuts.

The freshly rubbed meat is ready to be grilled or cooked!

All Purpose Dill Seed Rub

Boost your steak with vibrant, spiced flavors of this all-purpose dill seed rub. It also beautifully seasons chicken and pork meat cuts. Apply this unique rub minutes before grilling or cooking; you can also store it at room temperature for 12-14 days without sacrificing on its quality.

Prep. Time: 5 min.

Total Time: 8-10 min.

Yield: 6-7 tsp.

Ingredients:

- Paprika - 2 tsp.
- Ground coriander - 2 tsp.
- Dill seed – 1 tsp.

- Dry mustard - ½ tsp.
- Garlic, minced – 1 clove
- Black pepper and salt as required
- Cayenne pepper - ¼ tsp.

Directions:

Mix in all the rub ingredients in your mixing bowl to make the dill seed rub. Gently mix all ingredients using spatula or spoon to form an aromatic rub mixture.

Now, take your choice of meat cut and place it on a firm surface. Brush the freshly made rub on it; pat gently for the rub to stick onto the surface. Turn the meat cut and repeat to spice up its other side. Repeat with other meat cuts.

Let your meat cuts adequately season for more rich flavors for a few hours in your refrigerator. Take them out, as they are ready to be cooked or grilled!

Rosemary Thyme Rub

This special rub recipe represents an interesting balance of spicy and sweet flavors to make truly mesmerizing meat meals.

A spiced combo of rosemary, thyme, and celery seeds never fails to produce delicious dishes with well-balanced flavors for the whole family.

Prep. Time: 5 min.

Total Time: 8-10 min.

Yield: 1 cup/16 tbs.

Ingredients:

- Dried thyme - 1/4 cup
- Dried crushed rosemary - 1/4 cup
- Dry mustard - 2 tbs.
- Ground black pepper - 4 tsp.
- Salt - 4 tsp.

- Onion powder - 4 tsp.
- Ground cloves - 2 tsp.
- Celery seed - 2 tsp.
- Cayenne- 1 tsp.

Directions:

Mix in all mentioned rub ingredients in your mixing bowl to make the rosemary rub. Gently mix all ingredients using spatula or spoon to form an aromatic rub mixture.

Now, take your choice of meat cut and place it on a firm surface. Brush the freshly made rub on it; pat gently for the rub to stick onto the surface. Turn the meat cut and repeat to spice up its other side. Repeat with other meat cuts.

Let your meat cuts adequately season for more rich flavors for a few hours in your refrigerator. Take them out, as they are ready to be cooked or grilled!

Super Spiced Curry Rub

Your favorite meat cuts deserve a little jazzing up with this unique curry flavored rub. Paprika mixed with curry powder and cinnamon creates a perfect blend of spices. Be creative and add one or two of your favorite spices in it to come up with your own special version of spiced curry rub.

Prep. Time: 5 min.

Total Time: 8-10 min.

Yield: 10 tbs.

Ingredients:

- Ground ginger - 2 tbs.
- Yellow curry powder - 3 tbs.

- Ground cinnamon - 2 tbs.
- Salt - 1 tsp.
- Mild paprika - 1 tbs.
- Ground cumin - 2 tbs.
- Ground allspice - 1 tsp.

Directions:

One by one, mix in all mentioned rub ingredients in your mixing bowl to make the curry rub. Gently mix all the ingredients using spatula or spoon to form an aromatic rub mixture.

Now, take your choice of meat cut and place it on a firm surface. Brush or rub the freshly made rub on it; pat gently for the rub to stick to the surface. Turn the meat cut and repeat to spice up its other side. Repeat with other meat cuts.

Let your meat cuts adequately season for more rich flavors for a few hours in your refrigerator. Take them out, as they are ready to be cooked or grilled!

Mexican Cocoa Rub

Want to spice up your dry meats with savory Mexican flavors? Try out my classy rub this weekend. Cocoa and espresso powder are a special addition to this Mexican style rub creating soothing spiced aroma.

Prep. Time: 5 min.

Total Time: 8-10 min.

Yield: 9 tsp.

Ingredients:

- Water – 1 tbs.
- Cocoa, unsweetened – 1 tsp.
- Instant espresso powder – 2 tsp.
- Smoked paprika – 2 tsp.

- Olive oil – 1 tsp.
- Ground cumin – 1 tsp.
- Salt – ¼ tsp.

Directions:

One by one, mix in all the ingredients in your mixing bowl to make the cocoa rub. Gently mix all the ingredients using spatula or spoon to form an aromatic rub mixture.

Now, take your choice of meat cut and place it on a firm surface. Brush or rub the freshly made rub on it; pat gently for the rub to stick to the surface. Turn the meat cut and repeat to spice up its other side. Repeat with other meat cuts.

Let your meat cuts adequately season for more rich flavors for a few hours in your refrigerator. Take them out, as they are ready to be cooked or grilled!

Juniper Sage Meat Rub

This unique meat rub has been crafted with quality by including numerous healthy herbs such as juniper berries, lay leaf, red pepper, etc. It delivers piney accent to the rub, which ultimately enhances the flavor of your favorite meat cuts.

Prep. Time: 5 min.

Total Time: 8-10 min.

Yield: 8 tsp.

Ingredients:

- Bay leaf - 1
- Black peppercorns - 1 tsp.
- Juniper berries - 2 tsp.
- Extra-virgin olive oil - 2 tbs.

- Crushed red pepper - ½ tsp.
- Kosher salt - ½ tsp.
- Minced garlic – 1 clove
- Minced sage leaves - 6

Directions:

Mix in the bay leaf, red pepper, salt, peppercorns, and berries in your spice blender, grinder or processor to make the juniper rub. Start processing or grinding the mixed spiced on "pulse" mode to ground.

Empty the mixed spice mixture in a bowl; mix in the sage leaves, oil, and garlic. Mix again well.

Now, take your choice of meat cut and place it on a firm surface. Brush or rub the freshly made rub on it; pat gently for the rub to stick to the surface. Turn the meat cut and repeat to spice up its other side. Repeat with other meat cuts.

The freshly rubbed meat is ready to be grilled or cooked!

Southwestern Oregano Thyme Rub

This rub is a perfect blend of herbal, sweet, and earthy ingredients to make your day truly special and delicious. If you wish to make your meat cuts less spicy, then you can adjust the quantity of chili powder.

Prep. Time: 5 min.

Total Time: 8-10 min.

Yield: 11 tbs.

Ingredients:

- Garlic powder - 2 tbs.
- Chili powder - 2 tbs.
- Dry mustard - 2 tbs.
- Dried thyme- 1 tbs.
- Dried oregano - 1 tbs.

- Mild paprika - 1 tbs.
- Ground coriander - 1 tbs.
- Ground cumin - 1 tbs.
- Salt - 2 tsp.

Directions:

Mix all mentioned ingredients in your mixing bowl to make the oregano thyme rub. Gently mix all the ingredients using spatula or spoon to form an aromatic rub mixture.

Now, take your choice of meat cut and place it on a firm surface. Brush or rub the freshly made rub on it; pat gently for the rub to stick onto the surface. Turn the meat cut and repeat to spice up its other side. Repeat with other meat cuts.

The freshly rubbed meat is ready to be grilled or cooked!

Tangy Pepper & Thyme Rub

Transform your dry meats into full of citrusy, dark, and spicy flavors with this triple spice rub. The tangy thyme rub is quite easy to prepare and beautifully spices up your chicken, pork as well as beef.

Prep. Time: 5 min.

Total Time: 5 min.

Yield: 2 tbs.

Ingredients:

- Dried thyme - 1tbs.
- Lime zest, finely grated – 1 tbs.

- Sea salt and black pepper as required

Directions:

Mix in all the ingredients in your mixing bowl to make the pepper and thyme rub. Gently mix all the ingredients using spatula or spoon to form an aromatic rub mixture.

Now, take your choice of meat cut and place it on a firm surface. Brush or rub the freshly made rub on it; pat gently for the rub to stick onto the surface. Turn the meat cut and repeat to spice up its other side. Repeat with other meat cuts.

The freshly rubbed meat is ready to be grilled or cooked!

Amazing All-Season Fish Rubs

Oregano Cumin Tilapia Rub

This rub is a family-friendly way to savor an earthy, mild combination of spices in your favorite fish meals. The rub includes mild flavors, suitable even for children. Apart from Tilapia, it is also perfect for varieties of fish including salmon. Enjoy with mashed potatoes!

Prep. Time: 5 min.

Total Time: 8-10 min.

Yield: 4-5 tsp.

Ingredients:

- Light brown sugar – 1 1/2 tsp.
- Paprika – 1 1/2 tsp.
- Dried oregano - 1 tsp.

- Cumin - 1/2 tsp.
- Garlic powder - 3/4 tsp.
- Cayenne pepper - 1/4 tsp.
- Salt - 1 tsp.

Directions:

Mix in all mentioned ingredients in your mixing bowl to make the cumin tilapia rub. Gently mix all the ingredients using spatula or spoon to form an aromatic rub mixture.

Now, take your choice of fish and place it on a firm surface. Brush or rub the freshly made rub on it; pat gently for the rub to stick on the surface. Turn it and repeat to spice up its other side.

Let your fish cuts adequately season for more rich flavors for some time in your refrigerator.

*Do not let your fish season for more than 2 hours (but not less than 30 minutes).

Take it out, as it is ready to be cooked or grilled!

Spicy Sumac Rub

This special spicy rub perfectly complements different choices of fish; it adds up extra flavors to your fish-based meals. I mean, no one likes to compromise on the mild, mouth-watering taste of Tilapia.

Prep. Time: 5 min.

Total Time: 8-10 min.

Yield: 2-3 tsp.

Ingredients:

- Dried thyme - 1/2 tsp.
- Powdered sumac - 1/2 tsp.
- Any variety of Creole seasoning - 1/2 tsp.
- Onion powder - 1/4 tsp.
- Garlic powder - 1/4 tsp.

- Salt - 1/4 tsp.

Directions:

Mix all mentioned ingredients in your mixing bowl to make the spicy sumac rub. Gently mix all ingredients using spatula or spoon to form an aromatic rub mixture.

Now, take your choice of fish and place it on a firm surface. Brush or rub the freshly made rub on it; pat gently for the rub to stick onto the surface. Turn it and repeat to spice up its other side.

Let your fish cuts adequately season for more rich flavors for some time in your refrigerator.

*Do not let your fish season for more than 2 hours (but not less than 30 minutes).

Take it out, as it is ready to be cooked or grilled!

Lemon Pepper Coriander Rub

This intelligently created pepper coriander rub provides hints of tartness along with mild spiciness with inclusion of chili powder. A great choice of rub to flavor-up your weekend nights as well as any night you wish to make special.

Partner your fish meals prepared with this special rub with red wine for a truly refreshing meal time.

Prep. Time: 5 min.

Total Time: 8-10 min.

Yield: ½ cup + 3 tsp.

Ingredients:

- Chili powder - 1 tbsp.
- Lemon pepper seasoning - 1/4 cup

- Ground cumin - 1 tbsp.
- Light brown sugar, firmly packed - 1 1/2 tsp.
- Ground coriander - 1 tbsp.
- Kosher salt - 1/2 tsp.
- Ground black pepper - 1 1/4 tsp.
- Red pepper flakes - 1/2 tsp.

Directions:

Mix in all mentioned ingredients in your mixing bowl to make the lemon coriander rub. Gently mix all the ingredients using spatula or spoon to form an aromatic rub mixture.

Now, take your choice of fish and place it on a firm surface. Brush or rub the freshly made rub on it; pat gently for the rub onto stick on the surface. Turn it and repeat to spice up its other side.

Let your fish cuts adequately season for more rich flavors for some time in your refrigerator.

*Do not let your fish season for more than 2 hours (but not less than 30 minutes).

Take it out, as it is ready to be cooked or grilled!

Long Island Spiced Rub

Tickle your taste buds with a vibrant spice mixture of cinnamon, nutmeg, black pepper, and cloves. Fish meals spiced with this rub make perfect combo with your choice of fresh salad along with lime drink or juice; it is also a great choice to pair up with coconut and pineapple salsa.

Prep. Time: 5 min.

Total Time: 8-10 min.

Yield: 16-18 tsp.

Ingredients:

- Nutmeg - 2 tsp.
- All-spice - 1 tbsp.
- Cinnamon - 2 tsp.
- Ground ginger - 2 tsp.

- Garlic powder - 2 tsp.
- Ground black pepper - 2 tsp.
- Ground cloves - 1 tsp.
- Cayenne pepper - 2 tsp.
- Sugar - 1½ tbsp.
- Salt - 1½ tbsp.

Directions:

Mix in all mentioned ingredients in your mixing bowl to make the long island rub. Gently mix all ingredients using spatula or spoon to form an aromatic rub mixture.

Now, take your choice of fish and place it on a firm surface. Brush or rub the freshly made rub on it; pat gently for the rub onto stick on the surface. Turn it and repeat to spice up its other side.

Let your fish cuts adequately season for more rich flavors for some time in your refrigerator.

*Do not let your fish season for more than 2 hours (but not less than 30 minutes).

Take it out, as it is ready to be cooked or grilled!

Chapter FOUR
The Amazing World of Meat & Fish Super Sauces

Packed with mouth-watering, moist & complex flavors, the following collection of classic meat and fish sauces will surely tease your taste buds and will make you crave for the recipes again and again.

Amazing All-Season Meat Sauces

Super Salsa Sauce with Mint and Anchovies

This saucy recipe has always been my favorite evening charmer. This high-flavor salsa sauce is a perfect fit to dress up your favorite steaks, be it grilled, roasted or simply pan-fried. Enjoy a warm dinner meal with this cool mint-based sauce!

Prep. Time: 5 min.

Total Time: 8-10 min.

Yield: 2 cups

Ingredients:

- Parsley, finely chopped - ¼ cup
- Mint, finely chopped – ¼ cup

- Capers – 1 tsp.
- Chives, finely chopped - ¼ cup
- Garlic, crushed – 1 clove
- Anchovies, chopped – 4 pieces
- Olive oil as required
- Lemon juice as per you taste preference

Directions:

Mix the mint, chives, and parsley in your mixing bowl to make the salsa sauce. Then, add the anchovies, capers, lime juice, olive oil, and garlic.

Thoroughly mix all the ingredients using spatula or spoon to form a smooth sauce mixture. Enjoy the freshly made aromatic sauce as a dip with your favorite meal meals!

Mustard Mushroom Beef Sauce

Add a fair of special flavors derived from mushrooms and mustard to your beef cuisines. This perfectly crafted beef sauce is an ideal one to serve on festive parties and casual events.

Prep. Time: 10 min.

Total Time: 30 min.

Yield: Sufficient for 12 oz. beef fillets or tenderloin

Ingredients:

- Canola oil - 1 tbs.
- Mushrooms (make thin slices) – 8 oz.
- Shallot, finely diced – ½ piece
- Beef stock - 1/2 cup
- Red wine - 1/2 cup
- Black pepper and salt as required
- Dijon mustard - 1 tbs.

- Unsalted butter - 1 tbs.
- Flat-leaf parsley, chopped - 1 tbs.

Directions:

To make the mushroom beef sauce, combine the oil, shallots, pepper, sal,t and mushrooms in your medium-sized saucepan. Cook them for 3-4 minutes until they turn light brown.

Then, mix in the red wine and stock. Let the mixture boil gradually until it reaches its half quantity.

Now, mix in the mustard and butter; gently stir the mixture and cook for about 45-60 seconds. Top with fresh parsley. Pour the hot sauce directly over the oil fried or grilled beef. Enjoy warm!

Creamy Horseradish Chicken Sauce

Give your dry chicken meat meals a spicy, solid kick of the horseradish; this unique sauce is packed with the tart, mild flavors of mustard, and white wine vinegar. Tastes amazing with chicken fingers or breaded chicken.

Prep. Time: 8 min.

Total Time: 10 min.

Yield: 1 ¼ cup

Ingredients:

- Grated horseradish - 1/4 cup
- Sour cream - 1 cup
- Dijon mustard - 1 tbs.
- Kosher salt - 1/2 tsp.
- White wine vinegar - 1 tsp.
- Ground black pepper - 1/4 tsp.

Directions:

Mix all mentioned ingredients in your mixing bowl to make the horseradish sauce. Gently mix all the ingredients using spatula or spoon to form a smooth sauce mixture.

Place it to chill in the refrigerator. Let the ingredients rest for 3-4 hours. Enjoy the freshly made aromatic sauce as a dip with your favorite cooked or grilled chicken!

Creamy Peppercorn Steak Sauce

Made in no time, this classy, flavor-rich steak sauce deserves a place in your repertoire. Along with your warm welcome, entice your party guests with this elegant creamy sauce.

Prep. Time: 5 min.

Total Time: 10-15 min.

Yield: 1 cup

Ingredients:

- Chicken stock – 5 oz.
- Red wine vinegar - 2 tbs.
- Green peppercorns - 2 tsp.
- Double cream - 4 tbs.

Directions:

To make the peppercorn sauce, add the vinegar into your medium-sized frying pan. Let it simmer for a few minutes.

Then, mix in the stock. Let the mixture boil gradually until it reaches its half quantity.

Now, add in the peppercorns and crush some of them using a spatula or spoon; add the cream to the sauce mixture.

Gently stir it. Allow 1-2 minutes to simmer the mixture and become thicker. Pour the hot sauce directly over your choice of grilled or cooked steak!

Tangy Beef Oregano Sauce

Classy beef oregano sauce is the precious present from my first love, my mother; she handed it over to me with so much pride. Every time I miss her, I am never hesitant about making this sauce for dinner.

This juicy ground beef sauce tastes divine with any kind of spaghetti. Try it once and you will never be able to have spaghetti without this sauce!

Prep. Time: 10 min.

Total Time: 1 hour 15 min.

Yield: 7-8 cups

Ingredients:

- Onion, chopped - 1
- Ground beef – 16 oz.

- Garlic, minced – 4 cloves
- Diced tomatoes – 1 can of 28 oz.
- Green bell pepper, diced – 1 piece
- Tomato paste – 1 can of 6 oz.
- Dried oregano – 2 tsp.
- Tomato sauce – 1 can of 16 oz.
- Salt - 1 tsp.
- Dried basil – 2 tsp.
- Black pepper – ½ tsp.

Directions:

To make the oregano sauce, combine pepper, garlic, onion, and beef in your medium-sized saucepan. Cook the ground beef mixture until it turns light brown.

Then, mix in the sauce, paste, and diced tomatoes. Season the sauce mixture with pepper, oregano, and salt.

Gently stir it. Allow 55-60 minutes to simmer the mixture. Serve hot!

Spiced Black Bean Sauce

Want to know a secret to make your steak incredibly luscious and deeply savory? Try this unique Asian style black bean sauce and make your steak a delightful delicious affair. Added with mixed spices and soy sauce, this is a foolproof sauce for the whole family!

Prep. Time: 5 min.

Total Time: 10-15 min.

Yield: 1 ½ cup

Ingredients:

- Brown sugar - 1 tsp.
- Black beans – ½ can (around 7-8 oz.)
- Mixed spice powder - 1 tsp.
- Honey - 2 tsp.
- Tahini paste – 2 tsp.
- Grated ginger – 1/2 tsp.
- Red chili - 1
- Water - 5 tbs.

- Cider vinegar – 2 tbs.
- Soy sauce – 2 tsp.

Directions:

Put black bean in your spice blender, grinder or processor to make the sauce. Start processing or grinding the mixed spiced mixture on "pulse" mode to finely ground.

Then, mix in the remaining ingredients. Grind or process them all to create a smooth mixture.

Transfer the mixture into your saucepan of medium size. Allow 4-5 minutes to simmer the mixture to make it thick and glossy. Pour the hot sauce directly over your choice of grilled or cooked steak!

Cheesy Nutty Chicken Sauce

How would you like your chicken breasts dressed up with juicy Italian flavors tonight? Wait no longer; infused with lusty flavors of garlic, pine nuts and olive oil, this cheesy Italian style sauce will take your chicken, veggies as well as pasta meals to another level of deliciousness

Prep. Time: 10 min.

Total Time: 15-20 min.

Yield: 3 cups

Ingredients:

- Grated Parmesan - 1/4 cup
- Salt - ¼ tsp.
- Basil leaves, packed - 1 1/2 cup
- Ground black pepper - 1/4 tsp.

- Minced garlic - 1 tsp.
- Walnuts or pine nuts, toasted - 2 tbs.
- Extra-virgin olive oil - 1/2 cup

Directions:

Mix in pepper, basil, and salt in your spice blender, grinder or processor to make the sauce. Start processing or grinding the mixed spiced mixture on "pulse" mode to finely ground.

Then, mix in the remaining ingredients. Grind or process them all to create a smooth pesto.

Pour the hot sauce directly over your choice of grilled or cooked chicken breasts!

Peanut Coconut Cream Sauce

Decorate your dry chicken breasts with nutty, exotic flavors of this spicy cream sauce. Coconut cream and peanut butter add richness to the sauce as well as delivers a bright punch.

Prep. Time: 5 min.

Total Time: 15 min.

Yield: 2 cups

Ingredients:

- Red curry paste - 4 tsp.
- Coconut cream - 2 tbs.
- Chicken broth - 1 cup

- Lime juice - 2 tbs.
- Peanut butter – 1/4 cup
- Coconut milk, unsweetened – 1/4 cup
- Fish sauce of your choice – 1 tbs.

Directions:

To make the peanut butter sauce, combine the cream in your medium-sized saucepan. Heat it for about 1-2 minutes.

Then, mix in the curry paste and heat for 2 more minutes. Mix in the fish sauce, peanut butter, milk, and broth. Allow 10-12 minutes to simmer the mixture. Let it cool and mix in the lemon juice.

Enjoy the freshly made aromatic sauce as a dip with your favorite cooked or grilled chicken breasts!

Amazing All-Season Fish Sauces

Ginger Tomatino Saucy Feast

This tangy ginger sauce seems a simple one, but it can really surprise people with its unexpected yummy, complex flavors. Being a time saver, the tomato fish sauce gets ready in no time; be creative and experiment by adding some new ingredients based on your intuition and discover a new unique flavor every time.

Prep. Time: 10 min.

Total Time: 25-30 min.

Yield: 2 ½ cups

Ingredients:

- Onion, chopped - 1
- Cooking oil – 1 tbs.

- Chopped cilantro or parsley - 1/4 cup
- Grated fresh ginger – 1 tsp.
- Salt - 3/4 tsp.
- Tomato puree - 1 3/4 cups
- Ground black pepper - 1/4 tsp.

Directions:

To make the tangy fish sauce, combine onions, and oil in your frying pan of medium size. Cook them for about 2-3 minutes. Now, add the ginger; continue to cook for about 2 more minutes.

Add the puree and salt; cover the frying pan and allow 8-10 minutes to simmer the mixture.

Now, take your choice of fish pieces, add them to the hot puree mixture; cook for 10-12 minutes. Add the cilantro to the fish puree mixture.

Place the cooked fish pieces onto a serving plate and top them with the hot sauce!

Bercy White Wine Sauce

Originated from a small district of Paris, this wonderful Bercy white wine sauce is a truly wholesome sauce for fish as well as a variety of seafood. White wine and shallots create a saucy, savory combination mixed with basic fish velouté.

Prep. Time: 45-50 min.

Total Time: 60 min.

Yield: 2 cups

Ingredients:

To prepare the fish velouté:

- Fish stock - 3 cups
- All-purpose flour – 1 oz.
- Clarified butter - 1 oz.

To prepare the sauce:

- Chopped shallots - 2 tbs.

- Butter - 1 tbs.
- White wine - ¼ cup
- Chopped parsley - 1 tbs.
- Lemon juice as required

Directions:

To prepare this savory fish sauce, you need to make fish velouté first. Add the fish stock in your medium-sized saucepan. Let it boil gradually. Set aside.

Add the clarified butter into the same saucepan; let it melt gradually. Then, mix in the flour with the butter using kitchen spatula or wooden spoon.

Then, mix in the hot stock into the pan mixture; gently stir it with the flour mixture. Allow 25-30 minutes to simmer the mixture. Your smooth fish velouté sauce is ready now.

To make the fish sauce, combine the shallots and wine in your medium-sized saucepan. Let the mixture boil gradually until it reaches its half quantity.

Then, mix in the prepared velouté into the hot pan mixture; gently stir it. Add in parsley and butter; mix thoroughly.

Allow 8-10 minutes to simmer the mixture. Mix in lemon juice and enjoy it fresh!

Fresh Tarragon Parsley Sauce

Freshly prepared from reducing wine, this herb-filled fish sauce truly enriches your body from within. The healthy herbal combo of tarragon, chives, and parsley adds plethora of essential nutrients and makes your fish meal mouth-watering as well as nutritious.

Prep. Time: 5 min.

Total Time: 10-15 min.

Yield: 2 cups

Ingredients:

- White Wine Sauce - 2 cup

- Chopped chives - 1 tbs.
- Chopped parsley - 1 tbs.
- Chopped tarragon - 1 tbs.

Directions:

To make the herbal sauce, pour the white wine into your medium-sized saucepan. Let it boil gradually for a few minutes.

Then, mix in the herbs; gently stir it. Allow 1-2 minutes to simmer the mixture.

You can pour the hot sauce directly over your choice of cooked fish or you can serve it as a dip!

Normandy Nostalgia Sauce

Velvety, smooth velouté sauce takes crucial part in creating popular fish-based dishes. Chopped mushrooms mixed with silky egg yolk and heavy cream create a rich and buttery texture to make your dinner a memorable one.

Prep. Time: 10 min.

Total Time: 30-40 min.

Yield: 2 cups

Ingredients:

- Fish stock - ¼ cup
- Fish velouté - 2 cups
- Chopped mushrooms - ½ cup

- Egg yolks - 2
- Heavy cream - ½ cup
- Butter - 1½ tbsp.

Directions:

To make the fish sauce, combine butter and mushrooms in your medium-sized saucepan; let the mixture cook gradually for 4-5 minutes for the mushrooms to become soft.

Then, mix the stock and velouté in the hot pan mixture. Gently stir it. Simmer until it reaches 1/3 of its quantity.

Now, combine the yolk and cream in your medium-sized bowl. Thoroughly whisk the ingredients.

Then, mix the mushroom mixture (1 cup) in the bowl. Mix well and place it back into the saucepan. Allow 2-3 minutes to simmer the mixture. Enjoy it warm with your favorite cooked/grilled fish!

Conclusion

A dry meat or fish is nothing without a brush of savory marinades. In a way, it's like an injection of flavors. Similarly, rubs, glazes as well as sauces are true flavor boosters that can bring any food alive. Creating a flavorful blend of ingredients and heavenly delicious meals is a science and one must aim to master at it.

The book aims at gifting its readers a truly versatile collection of marinade, rub, sauce, and glaze recipes to transform their meal time into a memorable dining experience. I hope that you have enjoyed learning the secrets of the covered recipes to create flavorful infusion. Keep making delicious meals for your whole family and spread the love of cooking!

Thank you for giving your precious time to read this book. Best of luck for all your endeavors! Keep smiling!

Printed in Great Britain
by Amazon